Better Business Systems

**Advice to business people
wanting to save time and money
when planning a new computer system**

Ian P Johnson

Dedication

This book is dedicated to my wife Hazel who has patiently listened to me talking about my work for all these years. Now she can read about it as well.

Contents

Acknowledgements

This book would not have been possible without the projects I worked on and my fellow workers, both within project teams and as clients. Without the successes and failures we shared together I would not have learned so much. I hope that this book, which summarises my lessons learned from the clients' point of view, will help more projects on their way to successful on-time on-budget completion.

Ian P Johnson, May 2014

ianpjohnson@yahoo.com

Preface

My advice to business people planning a new business system is primarily to remember this - it's been done before. As you will learn, the first business information system, the Lyons Bakeries Valuation System, went live in September 1951. The project, including designing and building the hardware and software took just under 3 years. It would be interesting to know how long it would take to build the same system today.

The history of developing business systems stretches back over 50 years and during that period many businesses have faced the challenge of business system project cost and schedule overruns and systems not doing what was expected of them.

The author has been involved in the IT business for over 25 years, and has observed some of the successes and failures first hand. This book is about passing on the lessons learned from a business perspective.

The approach is, shall we say, anecdotal, with real world case studies used, with the names changed to protect the innocent.

All IT jargon is explained in footnotes.

Introduction

A new business system, business platform or business application can be a daunting proposition for many people in business. Defining the requirements for your new system, selecting a supplier to deliver it, and finally commissioning and training your team to use the new system may be completely new to you. Worse still you may have read, or been told of projects to deliver new business systems that cost far more than budgeted, or took far longer than expected to deliver. In the worst cases, the project might have failed, and the system not delivered at all. Unfortunately these scenarios are not uncommon in the IT industry, even today, with the industry's accumulated best practice knowledge of over 50 years.

As a business person rightly concerned with protecting your business's investment in the new system and increasing the likelihood of success, where do you turn? There are plenty of theoretical books on project management, and indeed plenty of best practice methods for eliciting requirements, designing systems, managing the project and managing the change to your business. These methods are essential but they do not provide the insight of actual practical experience. This experience is not easily obtained. Typical substantial business changing projects can take years, and to discern the patterns of success and failure requires experience of many such multi year projects.

This book gives you that business system project experience, in fast forward. By reading anecdotal examples of actual, typical project scenarios, you will get to experience the successes and failures of the world of business systems projects at a fraction of the time and cost. The common pitfalls are described in the same way, and finally, the book explains the lessons learned and the keys to success.

Let's begin by looking at three scenarios that a business person building a new software solution would face. "How much?", "How long?", and "It's under control!".

Situation 1 - How much?

At a large bank, The Anchor Bank[1], the program manager for the Mortgage Rapid Approval Program (MRAP)[2] is looking forward to receiving the estimated costs of building a new system. The software is a small component of an overall

---

[1] The Anchor Bank is completely fictitious, resemblance to a real bank is purely coincidental.

[2] The Mortgage Rapid Approval Program is a totally fictitious program.

program that will launch the bank's highly competitive online mortgage approval system. When released, the bank's mortgage broker partners will be able to obtain approval of mortgages for a client within 20 minutes of completing an online application. It is expected to reverse a slow decline in the bank's market share and as such MRAP is a pet project of the CEO.

The Bank's IT suppliers[3], Consultants-R-Us[4], arrive for a meeting with the program manager and the head of the mortgage business unit. They are represented by their project manager[5], solution architect[6], and account manager[7]. They have a presentation, and it follows predictable lines; our understanding of your requirements, how we will implement your requirements, alternatives we looked at, and cost and schedule.

---

[3] An IT supplier is an organisation that supplies computer software, hardware or services to a customer.

[4] Consultants-R-Us is a fictional IT services supplier.

[5] A project manager leads a project, and is responsible for scope, time, cost, quality and risk and leading the team. A project is a temporary organisation to deliver specific business products or changes to a customer.

[6] A solution architect is an IT professional whose role is take the business requirements and from these develop a high level design for the new computer system known as a solution architecture.

[7] Responsible for the overall relationship with the customer.

They all sit down, and the Consultants-R-Us project manager puts his USB key into the PC, and the presentation begins. The requirements are quite complex, as the system needs to be available 24 hours a days, seven days a week, without any down time, and the fraud checking and credit rating processes involve interfaces to many different organizations. Finally, the security implications are quite complex. Consultants-R-Us looked at several different approaches, but in the end was constrained by the bank's enterprise architecture[8], and the need for security. The Bank's executives are satisfied that Consultants-R-Us have understood what needs to be done.

The Consultants-R-Us team are not looking forward to the next part of the presentation. The account manager carefully watches the head of the mortgage business unit, as the project manager commences explaining how Consultants-R-Us arrived at the costs. Finally a slide appears that says at the top:

"The estimated cost of delivering the software solution is between $18m and $25m and the likely timeframe is 18 months."

Below this statement is a graphic that shows the

---

[8] The overall computer design principles in an organisation that define the organisation's standard approach to designing computer systems.

timeline.

"That's a lot more than we were expecting" says the head of the mortgage business unit. "Is there any way you can reduce the cost, and maybe deliver faster. Have you considered using iterative software development, or building it in India[9]?"

"This breaks our business case", says the MRAP program manager[10]. "At this price it will not be feasible, and in 18 months time we will have lost market share."

On the Consultants-R-Us side of the table no one is surprised, they have heard it all before. The architect thinks to himself, "Perhaps they just want us to change the slides, but in 18 months they will have paid $25m or maybe more. Why can't they be realistic? If they want a new business channel, using the latest technology, they should expect to pay for it."

The account manager says, "Can we come back with a more detailed explanation of how we arrived at the costs? Perhaps some parts of your requirements are higher priority than others. Maybe we can

---

[9] India is a real country in Asia with a large inexpensive IT workforce.

[10] A program manager is responsible for achieving specified business change, and usually has several project managers reporting to him.

deliver the highest benefits first?"

Situation 2 - How long?

Across the other side of the city, at a large
government department, the Ministry of
Licensing[11], a project control board[12] meeting of the
Bond Forfeit System Project[13] is taking place. The
project is making a change required by legislation to
a large complex system that manages citizens'
driving licenses. The legislation allows citizens who
are caught drunk driving to purchase the right to
put up a large bond that will be forfeited if they
repeat the drink driving offence. The software must
also improve the calculation of license validity
dates, and in particular must handle multiple
offenses, back dated offenses and concurrent
offenses.

The project has found itself in quite a challenging
position and has been explaining its problem

---

[11] The Ministry of Licensing is a completely fictitious government
department that licenses everything from pilots, to dogs, thereby
generating a large recurring revenue stream for the government.

[12] A project control board is a group of roles representing business,
users and supplier, to whom the project manager reports.

[13] The Bond Forfeit System is a fictional program that will enable
licensees to pay to avoid losing their licenses, thus generating even
more revenue for the government.

individually with the members of the project board. The software that calculates license renewal dates and the bond period is working correctly, however, there is a problem with the database[14] that holds the drivers' license information and the drivers' offenses.

The data has been converted to a new structure twice before, and has been subject to numerous manual modifications and as a result the project has discovered that the records cannot easily be converted again.

The Consultants-R-Us project manager is not looking forward to the meeting. Although he has a very good explanation of the problem, and how to solve it, he knows that the board will not like the proposal's cost even though he has softened them up.

The board believes that Consultants-R-Us uses every opportunity to request changes[15] that add to the cost and timeframe of the project, and that this is yet another example.

---

[14] A computer system that provides a structured store of data, from which data can be retrieved using something called structured query language (SQL). Oracle is a well known example.

[15] Changes on projects are known as change requests, and define the change, benefit and any associated change to time and budget.

The project manager begins, "We have completed the software and screen development on time, but have found challenges with the data conversion".

"The existing data contains numerous problems. There are drivers whose licenses have no start date, others with no end date. Some drivers have birth dates in the future, or dated before the invention of the motorcar, or even the invention of the wheel, or have no date of birth. For others, there is no evidence that they ever passed the test yet they have a full license. Some have so many offences that they will never be entitled to a license. Others have multiple licenses and we cannot tell which offense belongs to which license. There are offenses without licenses, and cancelled licenses without offenses. Worse still, when we apply the new license renewal date calculator to the newly converted data, the renewal dates do not match. The old calculator was wrong, so if we implement the new calculator, the system's renewal dates will not match those on the license."

The project executive asked, "Well, why not just change the new calculator, so that for existing licenses the date is the same as printed on the license."

"We can't do that, as we are required to implement software that follows the legislation. We cannot knowingly build something that is incorrect," replied the project manager.

"Well, Consultants-R-Us built the previous calculator", said another board member.

"Actually we did not, your previous supplier built it, and you tested it and approved it for implementation. I am not saying that we would have done any better", said the project manager.

"But surely the data problem is your responsibility, after all you have been the supplier here for over five years", the board member said.

"Yes, and no. Although we have converted the data, we are not the owners of the data, nor are we responsible for ensuring that it is correct. We have converted it according to rules you have supplied and was accepted by your test team. In addition there is the issue of the manual changes, which were undertaken by the Ministry of Licensing team."

The project manager continued: "The history got us to this point - what I would like to do is to propose a solution to the problem."

"Go on" said the project executive, whose own license records would not stand detailed scrutiny. "We want to solve the problem, not point fingers."

"I'd like to propose a four stage solution. We will

identify all the classes of license problems listed above, and determine with you how to convert the data, and then we will test the data to see if it converts and calculates correctly. For all those licenses that fail - we will repeat the process - we will try and identify the problems, define solutions and then convert and test. We will do this until all except a manageable number of rogue licenses are left."

"You will want to know how long this will take", continued the project manager, distributing a sheet of paper with an outline project plan - "we think each stage will take about three months, and we think that four stages will be needed. The cost of each stage will be about $250,000." He knew that this would not be popular, but had not found any alternative.

There was a long silence.

"So you are asking for another year and another million dollars on top of a $400k project. That's some blow out," said the project executive, "even for you lot."

"Yes, the alternative is that every driver in the state will have a license end date printed on their licenses that does not match the date that the computer generates.

Plus, there will be drivers on the road who should not be there, and drivers who should be back on the road who are prevented from getting a license. There is potential for a lot more adverse publicity," said the project manager, playing his trump card.

The Ministry of Licensing approved the revised project budget and schedule a few days later. There was not really any alternative.

Situation 3 - It's good to have a project under control!

The AML[16] Project is 95% complete, wrote the project manager in his project status report[17], and is expected to deliver on time and on budget just before Christmas. Although there were a number of issues, these all had satisfactory solutions that could be resolved within the project contingency budget. The major risk areas were performance and usability, however, previous systems had not experienced performance or usability problems, and there was no reason why this one would be any different.

---

[16] The AML project is fictional, although it is based on real legislation.

[17] A project status report, also known as a highlight report, describes the project's progress during a given period. It contains % complete, costs to date, earned value, risks and issues and a narrative description of progress.

The Anti Money Laundering Audit Project was intended to enable real time review of large retail transactions within the bank. It was needed to comply with anti-money laundering legislation. The idea was that all such transactions were identified and entered into a queue, and from there, transactions selected as suspicious by the rules engine were brought up on a screen within 10 seconds for central review before the customer left the branch.

The project executive often complimented the project manager on the steady progress of the project, unlike many of the projects run by Consultants-R-Us, who were always reporting problems. Wherever Consultants-R-Us project managers were to be found, there always seemed to be problems[18], issues[19] arising, risks[20] eventuating, blowouts, overruns, slippage, exception reports[21], in fact it was amazing that anything ever got

---

[18] In IT terms, a problem is a repeated incident or repeated defect.

[19] An issue is a difficulty on the project that needs to be addressed.

[20] A risk is a potential threat to project objectives that may occur in the future.

[21] An exception report is issued to a project board by the project manager when he forecasts that he will exceed tolerances of cost, schedule or quality that he or she is not able to resolve through corrective action.

delivered. He dreaded Consultants-R-Us's fortnightly detailed reports. Maybe more projects should be run in-house.

The project executive suggested a write up in the company magazine. There would be a picture of the project team smiling at the camera, with the project schedule pinned on the wall in the background, and the critical screen on the desk in the foreground. High risk transactions in the test system data would be highlighted in red and would be clearly visible in the photograph. We could even include the marketing girls in the foreground - they would be sure to catch the CEO's eye.

Meanwhile the project manager was applying for another job. There was no chance the project would deliver by Christmas or anytime soon. Although the software had been developed, it had been built to requirements created by the auditors. However, the auditors themselves could not, and would not, explain how they had arrived at and verified their requirements. For instance, did the requirements match the business process[22]? Whenever the project manager asked about this, he was told that he did not understand their business, it was the auditors' job to define the software requirements, and the IT department's job to build it. Independent review

---

[22] A written document, describing the steps that the business performs to deliver its products to its customers.

was out of the question. Then there was the issue of performance. Because of cost constraints, the system would run in production on existing hardware used to process transactions. Either the existing transactions would slow down, or the audit system would not meet its performance requirements.

When the project manager had tried to include this information in his report, it had been edited out by his boss, who told him that such comments were not what was expected of a team player.

The symptoms

Business people at all levels are familiar with the problems of IT projects. Costs are often higher than originally forecast, delays to delivery dates are common, and the system often does not do what it was originally intended to do.

Business people are often amazed by the changes to costs and date for a project, and often point to how their own business would suffer if they continually changed product costs and timeframe and even the product itself. Somehow, IT suppliers appear to live in another world.

Costs

Business people often find that costs of systems are higher than expected in a number of different ways.

Firstly, initially quoted[23] costs for new information systems or major changes are often far higher than anticipated. Business cases for new business products, that need to be supported by a new system are often thwarted by bafflingly high initial

---

[23] An estimate that a supplier provides to give an indication of likely costs.

estimated[24] costs. From a business perspective, suppliers often appear to be gold plating, or over engineering or simply price gouging. The example in the introduction, at the fictional Anchor Bank, is typical.

System development costs are often a puzzle for businesses, who don't understand how an IT supplier estimates costs. There must be many business people who think that a few fast programmers[25] could knock out the system for them in about three weeks. In some cases, they may have a prototype of the screens, put together by a contractor[26] in a couple of weeks, and want to know why their IT supplier is such a slow paced dinosaur. Sometimes even IT suppliers think this way as well. On one project, a web based superannuation front end[27], the functions were so simple, the scale so small, that it did seem like about three weekends' work for a hobby programmer, until you took into account the client's cumbersome enterprise

---

[24] An estimated price for a system that the supplier has determined through some estimating technique. Usually they come with a range of accuracy.

[25] The people who actually write the computer software code.

[26] Usually a specialist skilled programmer who is not an employee, but instead works by the hour on a fixed term.

[27] The part of the computer system that provides the user interface – such as the screens.

architecture. Ironically, despite being engineered to last five years at huge scale, the system was never used as the business never managed to sell a single superannuation plan in the target market.

Costs also typically escalate during the lifetime of the project. During the design stage of a project, additional costs are often identified as the design is elaborated in more detail. It's rather like the Mandelbrot set, the more detail you look at a problem in, the bigger it gets. Business cases that were initially acceptable, become less acceptable as design progresses.

During the build stage of a software project, the estimates for building components can often turn out to be under estimates, and indeed more components may be needed than originally envisaged. A series of requests by the supplier for more money to fund software to deliver the original requirements can be a source of significant frustration and management time.

During the business acceptance testing[28] stage additional costs may be incurred by the

---

[28] Also known as user acceptance testing or UAT, this is the final test, conducted by the business, that determines if the new system will go live.

identification of defects[29] that require significant changes to correct. The source of the defects may be in the requirements[30], or in the technical design[31]. If a defect is identified in the test stage[32], the costs of change will be higher than if it had been identified earlier, plus the impact on the business product launch will be far greater.

Delays

Delays to delivery dates for new software platforms are also a frequent cause of frustration. Delivery dates for software platforms are often connected into business product launches, or to release[33] dates for other software systems, or are constrained by seasonal demands on systems or by financial years.

---

[29] Errors introduced into a system that prevent the system working as intended. They can originate in any stage from requirements to writing the program code.

[30] The business requirements describe what the business wants. This is a formal document from which the system design is developed.

[31] The technical design is the document used by the programmers as a reference when writing the software programs.

[32] The test stage typically comprises system testing – does it work? integration testing – does it work with other systems? and user acceptance testing – does the end user agree that it works?

[33] A release is one or more changes to an IT system that are built tested and deployed together.

People planning a business product launch are often disconcerted that a project that was planned to deliver in a one year or longer time frame frequently proposes changes in dates. How is it that with such long timeframes, that IT suppliers are unable to keep their side of the bargain. After all, the business product side have produced the brochures, and booked the conference centre for the launch and even chosen the canapés and drinks. Why can't the IT supplier deliver the system on time? It can't be that hard.

The software does not do what was expected.

It's not uncommon for a software platform to fail to do what it is expected to do in some significant way. Despite careful requirements gathering, design, design reviews[34] and several stages of testing, software platforms often do not do what they are supposed to do, or don't do it fast enough, or cannot perform for long enough.

Something not working as expected often emerges once the system has gone live, and some key

---

[34] A design review is typically undertaken by the enterprise architects to verify that the system design is conceptually capable of working and is understandable, and that it satisfies the requirements and enterprise architecture.

functional activity cannot be performed. This often stems from the requirements, but the feeling is often that the supplier should have known about this and was expected to deliver this without being formally told.

Sometimes the software can do something that it should not, or people who should not be able to access the software can access it.

A common theme is that the system does not perform fast enough, particularly at peak periods.

Relationship between time, costs and quality

Costs, delays and software not performing as expected are equivalent in the world of projects to resources applied, timeframe and quality.

The relationship between time, costs and quality[35] are shown in the schematic diagram below.

---

[35] Quality means is the system fit for purpose, and does it satisfy requirements.

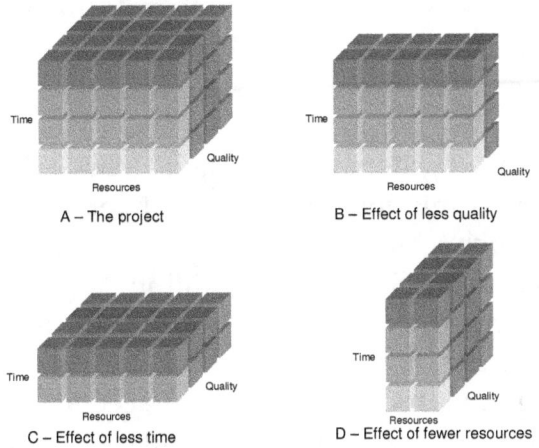

A – The project

B – Effect of less quality

C – Effect of less time

D – Effect of fewer resources

In this diagram, the volume of the cube represents the value of the system, in terms of its capability. If any of the three dimensions is reduced, then the volume of the cube, and hence its value is reduced.

In example B the quality has been reduced by half, reducing the value. In example C only half the time is available - reducing the value. In example D the resources have been reduced, also reducing the value.

Businesses and IT suppliers must manage these three dimensions to deliver value.

Your business is a long way from space exploration, but NASA has faced this same challenge. NASA developed several missions under the banner of faster, cheaper, better. This is analogous to the cube above - however as we can see, reducing all three dimensions reduces the overall value of the product, in this case the mission.

NASA spent $327 million developing its Mars Climate Observer mission. Imagine what you could do with that much... but back to NASA. Unfortunately for NASA, the $327 million investment delivered no return on investment, as a quality error meant that the spacecraft's software was operating in metric units, but the spacecraft hardware was calibrated in imperial units. A lack of resources[36] (cheaper) meant that they did not notice this error until too late (faster), and the spacecraft crashed into Mars (bang). Fortunately it was only government money...

NASA's Mars Polar Lander also failed - it is believed due to inadequate software testing and as a result hundreds of millions of dollars of value was lost, a result of poor quality caused by insufficient resources.

Faster, cheaper, better is not impossible, but there is a threshold limit below which it is not possible to go, for each type of technology and leadership. This lesson applies to all projects.

---

[36] Resources are skilled people, desk space, computers, software and anything else needed to get the job done.

Our changing world

"Hey everyone, do you want a free mug?" One of our programmers had just come back from a discussion with the business about a fine point of screen design. "I've got a whole box. Apparently they are not needed anymore, so we can have them." The mugs were to be a promotional give away for people ordering bulk oil from the proposed centralised call centre. The new call centre was going to be very advanced, and would enable people from a regional centre to be directed to a particular salesperson, who might share some affinities, such as the same regional accent. Consultants-R-Us's development of the call centre software had been slowed down (or "timeframe challenged" if you don't want to use the Anglo-Saxon) as result of a series of change requests. The change requests were from the business, as a result of observing the capabilities of emerging customer relationship management (CRM)[37] packages. In fact, online ordering was likely to completely supersede the call centre.

"I think you may find the OASYS[38] system is not

---

[37] CRM systems are typically used by call centres in large organisations to track their dealings with their customers through all business channels – phone, email , letter and in person.

[38] OASYS is the most commonly used acronym for new systems. Every company has an OASYS

needed either," said one new owner of a mug. And that later turned out to be true. They must have been letting us down gently.

Business does not stand still, and many businesses have embarked on custom build[39] IT solutions to support their unique business proposition, only to find that their business moves faster than their IT supplier. It's a frustrating position to be in. Often a business finds itself facing a new external competitive threat that invalidates its plans.

Banks found themselves losing out in the personal loan market to non-bank loan competitors who were delivering web based loan services directly to car dealers and other retailers. Those loan competitors captured the retail loan market through deployment of innovative new systems. Meanwhile, the banks were upgrading their branch based teller personal loan systems but failing to reach a key new competitive channel.

Smaller, nimbler competitors have challenged the banks in the more lucrative mortgage market. Insurance is now being sold direct by non-traditional insurers.

In each case, the banks' business people would have

---

[39] Custom build means a uniquely developed software system for one client. It's the opposite of package software.

realized what was needed to compete, and then most likely would have been told by the IT supplier that the release schedule and resources were tied up for the next two years.

You aim should be to be that nimbler faster company.

The nature of the problem

The business of building leading edge software within acceptable margins of cost, timeframe and quality is a very different one to the main business of many organizations. For instance, in a large bank, most executives are interested in marginal changes in banking profitability as a result of small changes in the product, such as improving customer service or better advertising or a superior interest rate. In one bank a senior executive, who was an actuary, once observed in a meeting, as a result of some quick mental arithmetic applied to new financial results, that the rate of rate of reduction in market share was increasing. This type of thinking is very different to the engineering specialisation of building computer software.

An analogy for this difference might be to try to build a toaster on your kitchen table. (Let's build a toaster and not be too ambitious and try and build a microwave.) The toaster needs to be able to toast two slices of bread, in about five minutes. It needs to be ready for use before friends come to stay in about six weeks, and the kitchen table needs to remain available for dining. The toaster needs to be adjustable, so that we can get the right degree of toasting. It must be safe, economical and aesthetically pleasing. Could you do this?

This is rather different to what you normally do in your kitchen. You'd need to finalise the requirements, then produce some outline designs, a proof of concept might be needed to get the right type of heating element wire and length. The components would need to be identified and found in electronics catalogues, and assembled and tested. It's a very different activity to that which usually goes on in your kitchen, which is the cooking and eating of food.

Imagine, if you will, a fish and chip shop owner, who, instead of buying a deep fat fryer, had to write a detailed specification for a fat fryer, including how it worked, and send this off to an engineering firm with no experience in the field, to produce a fat fryer for their business. Even worse, imagine if they then came to your premises and asked you to supply them with the materials and an arc welder. No doubt several versions would be needed at significantly greater cost than is incurred in the real world where commercial kitchen goods are available in a catalogue.

Building a complex technical system in a retail customer facing business is housing two different businesses under the same roof. It's a different business to yours, but it's still a business, and a complex, demanding one at that. After all, Google, Apple and Microsoft are businesses.

Sometimes people in the customer facing business equate the typically not very good IT help desk with the people building software systems. An example of this was brought home to me on one project when I was part of an expert witness team seconded to a large law firm. The lawyers were intrigued by our work on the client site business model and were fascinated by our approach. We learned a lot from them too. However it came home to me one day how different we were, and what the real perception of us was, when one of the secretaries asked if we could fix her printer. Being helpful I offered to take a look, but within a few seconds realized that she needed to call her help desk. "Isn't that what you do?" she asked.

This perception of a vast gulf between business and IT had obviously struck home to a technology partner at a large consulting form. He was leading an annual meeting of the technology practice, from the most junior levels up, when he said "I've got some news for you, you are all business people."

At the same consulting firm, one client's people were surprised to learn, after a visit, that the firm was a business with its own office and business plan and revenues and profits. They thought that somewhere we had "real" business people who did all that for us. Not so.

Business people are often disappointed that their IT supplier does not know all the details of their business. A quite common comment is that "You don't understand our business." Any attempt to defuse this by either demonstrating knowledge, or demonstrating that it's not needed to deliver the software as it's a different business is met with closed ears.

Building software is a business all of its own, but it's a different business. It's the business of software development and solutions delivery.

Does every business have this problem?

Every business has this problem with the delivery of IT solutions even if their business is IT. While working at one major IT consulting form, I was amazed to learn that one of our clients was Microsoft. It seemed that even Microsoft saw the provision of its own internal IT systems as a different business to their own. After all, Microsoft said, "We make Microsoft software products, we don't know what you do with them!"

The grass is always greener on the other side of the fence

Imagine the scene at a major oil company's annual employee conference. Each department has a stand to show what it does, and a slot on the stage to explain what it does to the rest of the company. Towards the end of the conference, the CEO asks different departments to stand up and be applauded by the rest of the company. Exploration stand up to applause, then refining, then marketing, then tax (very important in an oil company). Toward the end, it's the IT department's turn for a standing ovation. About half the company stands up. Applause starts but then peters out unexpectedly. There is stunned silence from the oil men as they realize that half the employees in the room are from the IT department. What do they do all day long? They don't drill for oil, that's for sure. Not long after, looking for a quick fix, the CEO outsourced[40] the IT department.

Businesses faced with the need to deliver IT systems faster, cheaper and better often consider a number

---

[40] Outsourcing is replacing services, in this case IT services, provided by a corporation's own employees with services provided by an external company.

of alternative approaches to improving delivery. Some businesses look to a new supplier, some want new hardware, or a new methodology[41], or a new organisation, or a new management fad, or a completely new technology. But a quick fix is not always the answer.

A new supplier

"Is it possible to reduce the cost from the $3.2million you have quoted?" asked the project executive.

"Well, not with the requirements you have provided. What we did was to take your requirements, construct an outline software model[42] called a use case diagram[43] and then classify each of the use cases according to its complexity. We are able to estimate the cost of your software requirements directly from the number and complexity of the use cases, to within 30%. We do the estimate using an industry standard model that we have calibrated to our own projects. So we are

---

[41] A standardised process or series of steps for performing a process. Typical examples in IT are PRINCE2 for project management or ITIL for service management, or TOGAF for enterprise architecture.

[42] A conceptual model of a system. The Unified Modeling Language (UML) methodology provides a set of standards for software models.

[43] A use case diagram shows the set of use cases and actors (people using or affected by the system) and their relationships. It is a part of UML.

confident that based on your requirements and the enterprise architecture, that it is as accurate as you will get."

"We still see this as too expensive," said the project executive. "Our own consultant has created a prototype of the screens in two weeks, and thinks that we could save money by getting software houses to bid for individual components online. We think it could be done for a lot less than a $1 million. Our man has some innovative ideas for doing it cheaper and faster, in ways that you may not have considered. Maybe you should talk to him."

"Tell you what", said the Consultants-R-Us partner, "We'll do that, if you do this. Put it out to tender. We'll bid, and you select the lowest bid that you consider able to do the work."

The client packaged up the requirements as a tender, and got four bids, three for about $3.5 million, and one for about $400,000 from a company no one had ever heard of.

Consultants-R-Us heard about this through the grapevine and were not surprised when they were awarded the contract. The client lost about four months and the costs of the tender on both sides.

Back at head office, a Consultants-R-Us associate partner was doing a post implementation review of a project to implement an online banking system (this was some time ago). Consultants-R-Us had bid for the work, and had put in a bid of around $25 million. This was seen as an outrageous sum by the bank, which had instead gone with another supplier who estimated about $5 million. About six months later, with the project going pear shaped, Consultants-R-Us was invited to take over the project management of the project. About a year later, with the project completed, Consultants-R-Us, as project managers were in possession of the complete costs of the project. The total cost was just over $25 million, almost identical to their original bid. The client could have retained Consultants-R-Us and saved themselves some time, and time of course, is money.

Organisations change over time, and sometimes changing your IT supplier is a valid way to improve delivery. Offering a lower price is not the main criteria for choosing a new supplier. That lower cost supplier must also be able to explain what they are doing differently that enables them to offer the lower price. Obviously, if they are not able to explain the lower price, they may have a strategy to increase the price later, or worse still, they may not realize that they have under priced.

New hardware

Could new hardware be the answer?

Computer manufacturers have been designing, building, and selling new computers for half a century. Each new machine needs to be marketed and the effort involved in creating the marketing spin can be significant.

Back in the 1980s, Apple produced a brilliant advert for its early Apple Mac computers - it showed some dynamic consultants producing a report for their client using their new Apple Mac computers that could do word processing, create graphics, run spreadsheets. The Apple ended with one of the old guys saying to a colleague - "Why can't our computers do that?"

Soon everyone wanted a Mac, and even I had one on my desk, but I could not really see why it was any better than the IBM[44] clone I used every day. It was certainly a lot more expensive. I quite liked the cerulean blue of the screen background.

Right now the latest twist to new hardware is - that's right - no hardware at all. Cloud computing is the latest twist. By using the latest server

---

[44] The largest computer services and manufacturing company.

virtualization[45] technology combined with outsourced off site server farms[46], businesses can get rid of their servers all together. Written in invisible ink is the suggestion that you can get rid of your IT department, too.

"We need to migrate away from our HP 8400[47] boxes, the licenses are up for renewal next year, and the cost will impact how we allocate our budget," explained the project manager. "We plan to migrate to low cost virtual servers, and we need a plan, schedule and costs for migrating the applications. Our total budget is $500,000."

The Consultants-R-Us account manager was somewhat surprised. To migrate the client's entire business systems onto a new platform was likely to cost millions, and that excluded the cost of the new virtual servers, and the cost of operation. It soon came to a head, when it was realized that the cost of continuing to license the existing servers over the next five years was cheaper than the five year cost of virtualization.

---

[45] Vitualisation of a hardware computer server is a software version of a server on a much larger server. Typically several virtual servers can be hosted on a single physical server.

[46] A computer room full of servers.

[47] A Hewlett Packard Intel powered server.

This is a great example of a standstill migration - a lot of work and expenditure that results in no change to business capability. It's rarely worth it.

Another client had migrated to virtual servers. In this case the applications were compatible and so the migration was reasonably straightforward. The outcome was lower cost, more flexibility, but lower performing servers, a case of cheaper, better but not faster.

Cloud computing might be the answer, however, the cost of migration is likely to be expensive. It's not likely to be the solution to your problems.

A new methodology

"We should be using CASE tools," was the frequent refrain over lunch. (CASE means "computer aided software engineering") This was the 1980s when CASE tools were the latest fad. "Combined with a formal methodology which is a part of the tool, we would be sure to get our developments moving faster." Somehow I doubted this - it seemed what was lacking was the business reason for the new systems. Not only that but the CASE tool enthusiast didn't seem to be able to apply the same logic to his lunch. Despite the lunch being free[48], this being an oil company, all he ever ate was meat and potatoes, and was easily the unhealthiest person I had ever seen. If he couldn't make good judgments about his food, how could he make good judgments about anything?

Some years later I found myself working at a CASE tool vendor. You've probably never hear of CASE as it has become almost completely obsolete, mainly because of the $50k per seat license cost of the software, and the rise of low cost software development houses in places like India. What CASE did was to enable a software engineer[49] to create a data model[50], a process model[51], an action diagram[52] and then push a mouse around to create some pseudo-code[53] and then generate the

---

[48] In fact local pensioners used to sneak in for a free lunch, pretending to be employees.

[49] Software engineers apply the principles of engineering to the design, development, maintenance, testing, and evaluation of the software and systems that make computers or anything containing software work.

[50] A standardised model of the data in a database showing its composition and relationships.

[51] In this context a diagram showing the processes within the computer system and their relationships.

[52] An action diagram was a tool in the Information Engineering software method.

[53] High level code that represents compilable program code.

compilable code[54] for the client's machines. It was popular for large utility businesses, and had numerous advantages in terms of speed of development and platform independence. CASE was not popular with software developers, who doubted that their work could be automated, and when they found it could, voted with their feet. They preferred the Microsoft view of software development, or the open source[55] approach. Both were easier to work with and had far lower costs of entry and retained the developer's professional standing.

One client at the CASE tool vendor was renowned for the chaos that they brought to everything. I was privileged to spend a couple of days there to look over their design model. Despite having an industry leading CASE tool with advanced data modeling capabilities, they had created the worst possible data model, based on their existing system. The CASE Tool would only allow a correctly constructed model following the rules to be created, but it was the most illogical, inelegant and just plain confused data model I had ever seen. The processes too were as bad. However, the CASE tool built correct code and a database following this model

---

[54] Computer program source code, written by a programmer, that can be compiled into a software program that will run on a computer.

[55] Software for which the owner has made the source code available to others.

and the system worked just fine. Well, sort of. It was too slow and they wanted to know what we could do to speed it up. There was not much I could recommend except scrap it and start again. It was a miracle that it worked at all.

The new tool and methodology had not delivered any significant improvements from a business perspective, in fact, may even have made things worse.

Often new methodologies or tools are promoted by employees wanting something new to put on their CV, or who are just plain bored.

While a new methodology might be part of the solution it is not a silver bullet, and requires significant effort to implement and exploit effectively.

A new management fad

"I think we'll hold the meeting in the Emmental Room," I said, referring to one of the client's meeting rooms on its conference centre floor. The client had named its meeting rooms after famous cheeses[56]. I had no idea how to pronounce emmental so I

---

[56] I'm not making this up, believe me.

always pronounced it "mental". How did the client come to name its meeting rooms after cheeses? After all, it could have just given them numbers

It turned out a big cheese[57] in the client's management development training department had read the management fad book "Who moved my cheese?" After the success of the "One minute manager", Spencer Johnson, who co authored the One minute manager with Ken Blanchard, had sought to build on his previous success with a book about change. Designed to be distributed within corporations about to undergo major change, Johnson[58] hit the big time with "Who moved my cheese?" Over five million copies have been sold, although it is doubtful if anyone has read it from cover to cover. Most people gave up after the first few paragraphs reading about mice looking for cheese.

Designed to enable corporations to facilitate change, the book spawned numerous parodies and was very hard to take seriously. Any corporation attempting to use it to soften up its employees for a big change inevitably made matters worse.

Improving your IT delivery with a management fad

---

[57] Sorry, I couldn't resist it.

[58] No relation.

is likely to have the opposite effect.

Reorganisation

The only incorrect part about the following quote is that it's supposedly fiction:

"We trained hard, but it seemed that every time we were beginning to form up into teams, we would be reorganized. I was to learn later in life that we tend to meet any new situation by reorganization; and what a wonderful method it can be for creating the illusion of progress while producing confusion, inefficiency and demoralization."

Supposedly written by a certain Petronius Arbiter in the 1st century AD, during the time of Nero, Petronius was an early satirist, who has had this quote hung around his neck like an albatross. The false quote appears to stem from the 1950s[59] but resonates with many people. I've reproduced it here to help set the record straight and to help pad out this book.

Can it be true that reorganization achieves nothing? After all, it's often the same people doing the same jobs, but with a different organisation chart. If this is

---

[59] At least that's what it says on Wikipedia.

all your re-organisation is, then evidence is it will achieve nothing. A reorganization that works requires an accompanying change to the business process, which is required to better satisfy customers.

Does it really matter what technology we use?

Back in the 1950s in the UK, the Lyons Tea company decided to make their own computer in order to bring automation to their light refreshment business. They based their design on the Cambridge University EDSAC computer, and built the computer from scratch, ordering their own components, including valves, relays, wire, mercury delay tubes for storage etc. The Bakery Valuations Application went live in November 1951 after just two months of what would now be known as user acceptance testing[60]. Not long after they took on Ford's payroll system, the first known instance of outsourcing, and even started doing climate modeling for the UK Meteorological Office[61].

---

[60] User acceptance testing is the final test, conducted by the business, that determines if the system meets expectations and is ready to go live.

[61] And probably narrowly missed discovering global warming.

But this was before I was born, I imagine you are thinking[62]. What's this got to do with delivering faster, cheaper, better in the 21st century? Well just this - if Lyons could enter the outsourcing business in the 1950s using technology based on string and sealing wax, the technology you are using is probably not as important as what you do with it.

"We are not building a man hours system," the CIO was adamant. "Every year someone comes to me with a proposal to build a man hours system and I say, why do we need another one? We must have 20 already." He had a point. This was the research centre of a major oil company. Each research branch had a need to record and process man hours for each of its internal clients. The need for automation was apparent, and each branch used its in-house programming skills to build one.

There were man hours systems that ran on data logging computers and programmable calculators. The Applied Physics Branch had one written in FORTRAN[63]. Analytical Sciences used a punch card and assembler system. The Stores Department had one written in COBOL[64], the Secretarial Services

---

[62] It was also before I was born.

[63] FORTAN - A computer language used for mathematical modeling.

[64] COBOL – a computer programming language used for writing business systems. Not used as much as it once was.

department had one that used Wang[65] word processor macros. Exploration Branch notoriously ran their man hours system on a Cray[66] supercomputer. Another branch used DEC DCL[67], and yet another had a Unix[68] shell code[69] based system. The Accounts Team used a spreadsheet. In fact, the only department that did not have its own man hours system was the IT Department, where permission was needed to do anything useful.

"If we write a man hours system it will not satisfy all requirements, and it will be a rod for our own back," said the CIO. "Diversity is better, it's like evolution, and eventually the fittest man hours system will survive and out-compete the others." He had a point, and it fitted in with the IT department philosophy of "the less work we do, the less money we waste,"[70] and so, it never got built.

---

[65] Before personal computers, Wang made a purpose built word processor.

[66] Cray – a manufacturer of supercomputers named after Seymour Cray. Cray supercomputers were fast but expensive.

[67] DEC DCL was the operating system control language of DEC, a major manufacturer of minicomputers in the 1980s.

[68] Unix is the name of a widely used computer operating system, used in servers, desktop machines and even mobile phones.

[69] Shell code is the operating system control language of Unix. Legendarily cryptic.

[70] This same CIO even considered giving us all 6 months off on paid leave to save money.

For most business systems, it does not matter what technology you use, if there is a will there is a way. If someone is proposing a big technology change to solve a problem, it may not be the solution you need.

The IT suppliers' perspective

Some years ago a friend described an experience he had when buying a small business. They had engaged a solicitor who specialized in the sale and purchase of small businesses. The solicitor's role was to ensure that the title to the business, its intellectual property and capital assets were transferred to new ownership. It was the sort of thing he did all the time, liaising with the vendor's solicitor.

The negotiations for the sale had started well, but questions had started to arise about who owned some of the intellectual property. The vendors wanted to retain some of it, and this looked like it would need to be replaced by the new owners. There were lengthy discussions about this by the two parties.

The solicitor was not an expert in the business, nor was he trained in negotiation, his job was transfer of company title. Yet his many years of being present during the final stages of a company sale had given him a lot of knowledge about the behaviour of people selling their small business. He knew that they were often reluctant to let it go completely and would often try and retain something in which they had a lot of personal investment.

His advice was to insist it was all to be part of the sale, and then during negotiations let them keep one thing that they obviously found it hard to part with, but which would not significantly impact the future of the business. Following that advice the sale was agreed within the hour.

"He really earned his money through that advice," said my friend, "although negotiation was not part of his job, he saw many business sales during his career, yet the vendors and purchasers might only be in that situation once or twice in their careers."

This is a lesson with applicability in other fields, and especially in the field of building systems.

As business people with commercial expertise in your field, be it banking, manufacturing, or mining, or government, you understand what business system platforms are needed. But in your career, how many times will you commission a new system? Your IT suppliers' people may see a hundred or more new systems commissioned over the duration of a career, and taken collectively within their business this could be many thousands. Being present at each stage of the software development lifecycle[71] on many occasions provides

---

[71] The software development lifecycle, or SDLC, is the complete set of processes to turn requirements into a working system.

a unique perspective of the commissioning of business systems platforms, similar to that of the solicitor in the example above.

A number of repeating scenarios are often experienced by IT suppliers. These are - the client that cannot afford what it wants, that cannot prioritise across the enterprise, that does not recognize risk, that does not understand what they want, does not like the IT supplier asking questions and becomes emotionally charged when confronting these issues. This can happen at various levels of organization.

Many business people are able to handle these issues, but a significant minority are not.

"You want us to estimate based on that?" The project manager had produced a single side of A3 paper with a high level list of system requirements. The architect had recently successfully built a major teller system for the bank and had a reputation the envy of just about every other solution architect in Australia.

"You can't be serious," the architect said - "why not go away and produce a draft set of requirements. It would only take a couple of weeks!"

"We do not have time, as we have to create the costs for the business case by next week" said the project manager.

"But you do realize that we can only provide very approximate costs," said the architect.

"Yes, I know it's a bit unusual, but we have warned the project executive of the significant risk he is running and that further elaboration of the architecture or requirements may result in significant increase in costs."

This project highlighted the unusual estimating approach of the project executive. The project executive was an ex-McKinsey consultant and looked down on many of the bank's employees, especially in the IT department and IT supplier. He wanted a fast paced agile[72] project moving far more quickly than usual. He did not want old style methodologies and project processes getting in the way of progress. He saw himself as a high-powered intellect working with a team of donkeys.

"The risks are significant," explained the project manager. "What we are doing is using ball park costs in a detailed business case. Usually we use ballpark costs like this to establish that it is worth proceeding with a business case. Then we develop

---

[72] Agile – a software development method characterised by developing software iteratively in a series of short sprints, incrementally building the solution.

more detailed costs based on a high level architecture and requirements. During this stage it is likely that the elaboration stage[73] will identify more requirements or architectural components. We will need to include a significant contingency."

Unfortunately, this risk contingency[74] allowance was omitted from the costs of the business case. At a later stage the project manager advised that a risk in the risk log regarding additional components and costs had eventuated. An additional significant system component was needed in order to achieve the project objectives of platform independence[75]. Unfortunately, this cost was estimated at nearly $5 million, a significant sum, even on a $50 million project.

The project executive was incensed. "You can take your $5 million and your data broker[76] and write it on a piece of paper and flush it down the toilet!" The project manager could not believe what he'd heard,

---

[73] A stage used in some SDLC methods that elaborates from high level artefacts to detailed artefacts.

[74] A budget amount used to fund mitigation actions in the event a risk eventuates.

[75] Platform independence would mean that a software business system could run, or easily be made to run, on any computer operating system or virtual machine.

[76] The data broker translated system interfaces from differing software systems, and even changed the timing of the data.

but at the same time, the business system needed the data broker. The project executive's emotions were not the project manager's problem.

Some weeks later at an architect review meeting the technology for the data broker was under discussion for a decision on the technical direction. This was a joint meeting of the bank's IT architects and the project board. The project manager had been advised to continue with the data broker design. Eventually, during the meeting the subject was raised.

"Did we not decide to cancel this component?" asked the project executive.

"Well", said the project manager, "this is the component that you wanted to flush." Later in the meeting the bank's solution architects underscored the importance of the data broker. Without it the project would not succeed.

This was a great example of an angry client refusing to face the reality of what was needed to do the job and refusing to face the real costs. Fortunately, not a common occurrence, but this happens repeatedly.

The same project executive was also frustrated with the escalating costs of the security component of the system, which had been under-estimated for the same reason. Inside three weeks he sacked three successive chief security architects[77].

The IT supplier was unable to help as the project executive would not entertain the idea that the IT supplier understood how to estimate, how to architect, how to create a business case. The supplier's expertise, and that of the IT department and project, were not used. Eventually the project executive resigned to avoid being fired.

---

[77] A security architect is responsible for the overall design of the system security and identity and access management.

Facing reality

Sometimes computer systems are just too expensive for the benefits that they may offer. But that does not mean that the business, or the platform cannot proceed. Sometimes, it is possible to proceed without a business system.

I was hiring a car for the weekend and, as I did so, I noticed to my surprise that my credit card was put through an old-fashioned zip zap machine. Behind the counter was a long white board with a number of columns and a hook for keys at the top of each one. Each column showed the availability of each car, and who had booked it. "Do you use computers?" I asked, baffled by the lack of screens behind the counter.

"No, the boss thinks computers are a waste of money. This board here lists our cars, we park them out there in the order on the board. We can instantly see our cars availability, both on the board, and in the car park. He likes things simple. You can also see that all the cars are the same model, and the same colour. They even have consecutive number plates."

As a software development project manager, I was amazed. Car rental was an early application for computers. In fact, a demonstration system of one computer manufacturer's database system was a car rental system[78].

No doubt if this business had brought the consultants in, it could easily create a business case for a new car rental business system. But the business owner had a better business case - he was making more money without a computer based rental system.

During the dot com boom I was working for a large consulting firm. During the height of the boom I provided the costs for numerous business cases for various online services. In nearly every case the costs did not justify the likely revenue, and many business cases proved that there was no case for a particular business.

A business case that demonstrates that a particular business is not viable is still a useful business case document, as it stops your business wasting money. If your competitors are rushing into the market with the same platform, perhaps you know something that they don't.

IT suppliers often find themselves under pressure to try and reduce costs to make a business case fly, but usually, if the business case is marginal at the

---

[78] DEC's Datatrieve. They also offered a wombat database as an example.

outset, it is not worth pursuing

Sometimes a cheap and cheerful alternative is a good solution, at least in the interim, if you want to try a new business. Sometimes the cheap and cheerful solution is the answer. May I provide an example of a cheap and cheerful solution from a different industry?

On the A40 highway just outside London, the road passed over a low hill near Uxbridge, on the hill was a set of traffic lights at a junction with the B483. The lights caused enormous delays to traffic. Eventually work started to replace the traffic lights with a flyover and roundabout. During construction, temporary works were created that included a roundabout with traffic lights at peak times to ensure that traffic on the smaller road got an opportunity to cross. The temporary roundabout completely solved the problem, including at rush hour. The expensive flyover went ahead, but it was a major embarrassment. The temporary roundabout was a cheap and cheerful solution that satisfied motorists and would have saved taxpayers a fortune.

Back at the Anchor Bank, the project executive of the Anti Money Laundering Audit system was discussing the audit rule requirements with the project manager. The project manager was somewhat baffled by the lack of details concerning the rules for picking out transactions to be audited.

"We want an audit system with a flexible rules system that will enable us to pick out any type of transaction. For instance, if a bikie comes into our branch in Gingin with more than $10,000 in cash and deposits it into a newly created bank account, we would see that as suspicious and needing to be flagged."

"Do you have a list of the current rules you would use if you had the system?" asked the project manager.

"No, we will devise the actual rules once the system is operational," said the project executive.

"As there is a requirement for this system there must be a set of circumstances that you are looking for right now. We could turn those into rules and use them to validate the requirements."

"We don't have the rules at this stage."

"Would it take long to develop them?" It was clear to the project manager that the requirements for the system, in effect the outline design, were not backed up by any actual concrete business requirements, or even any kind of vision for the requirements beyond the apparent desire for rules.

The project manager proposed a cheap and cheerful system. Instead of building or buying a rules engine, a huge database, and a series of complex screens, all the transactions would be written to a file for a specific branch, and then the auditors would turn this into a spreadsheet and filter the transactions to look for suspicious activity. Once they had experience doing this manually they would have the experience to write the requirements. Who knows, the spreadsheet might even be sufficient.

The project executive was not keen on this spreadsheet approach, as he was concerned that the cheap and cheerful system might end up being the permanent solution. He did not want to be left with a half-built system, and was concerned that he would not be able to make a business case for completing the system.

The full system was built, but did not meet expectations, as the auditors found that the rules did not work as expected. About $1m was wasted. Had they taken the cheap and cheerful solution first, they could have created an elaborate set of business rules from which to formulate the types of rules that they needed to implement. This would have enabled them to produce more accurate requirements - their million dollars could have been spent on the system they knew they wanted, rather than the one they just thought they might need.

Businesses also find themselves in dilemmas over whether to proceed or not. A superb dilemma presented itself at a client that had been unsure of which technology platform to build its workflow system on. The client's enterprise architect had set a technical direction based upon Sun's[79] workflow[80] technology. However, the business was convinced that the Oracle[81] workflow solution was the better way to go. To resolve this difference of views, it was agreed to undertake a proof of concept. This was successful, and demonstrated that the Sun workflow solution was able to do the job. Shortly after, Sun was taken over by Oracle. Oracle announced that the Sun workflow system would not be enhanced and would be discontinued in a five-year timeframe. The client was left with a finely balanced decision that created a real dilemma as to which way to go. In the end the decision was made to continue with the Sun workflow system, as no system could be predicted to have a life of more than about five years.

---

[79] Sun is a major vendor and the owner of the Java technology platform.

[80] Workflow is a specialised system that automates the coordination of the process steps that a number of roles need to undertake.

[81] Oracle is a major vendor, and as of early 2010 now the owner of Sun.

Decisions about proceeding with business cases are often made with the supposition that the business case should go ahead. After all, otherwise we would not have spent time and effort building a document to prove that it is viable.

When writing a business case, the real possibility that the business case will tell you not to proceed should be kept in mind. Part of the challenge with this is communicating this reality at increasing levels of the business as the business case progresses.

Business cases should be commenced on the understanding, communicated upwards, that the outcome may tell you not to proceed.

Do you understand your own business?

"Of course I understand my own business", you are bound to respond, "it's our IT supplier who does not understand our business. If only they did understand our business, we would not get these frequent problems."

As mentioned earlier, your IT supplier's job is to understand their business, which is the delivery of business systems, and your business is to understand your own.

"You don't understand our business," I was told when attempting to challenge the client's understanding of a system design. The business concerned was boat inspections. After moving interstate, both my vehicles had been inspected at the client's facility, little did I know I would eventually be more professionally involved.

Back in the UK I had a keen interest in old boats, and had owned several old boats. Each boat had to be inspected on an annual basis. As these older boats were prone to fail the inspections, after attending several inspections I soon learned how to do the inspection, and understand what could be done in the event of an apparent failure. I even started pre-testing friends' boats to save them the cost of a failed inspection. I'd even had one of my old boats inspected when I moved it to Australia.

Being a great believer in understanding any business I worked for, we did attend a requirements gathering session at the boat inspection station, read the requirements in detail and attended demonstrations of the system as a work in progress. We had also undertaken a statistical analysis of the outcome of boat examinations that we felt was needed to understand the requirements.

After offering this information, it became clear that the business leader himself was not very interested in boats, or boat inspections, quantitative analysis, the process of boat inspections, process improvement or how the requirements for a new system might be gathered and put into action.

It was a puzzle with such leadership how the system would ever succeed. It was eventually delivered some years late. Of course this was fault of the IT supplier for not understanding the business!

History is written, it is said, by the victor, and a similar process occurs in corporations. History is written by the most senior people, and in the case of systems development it is the project executive commissioning the system that has the last word. The blame for many a delayed, failed or abandoned system development is laid at the door of the IT supplier. Many organizations are now following a post implementation review[82] process to obtain an objective view of the successes of the project, and the lessons learned.

At a merchant bank, an equities research system development was significantly delayed. The purpose of the system was to enable research analysts to maintain their forecasts of company results in a standard spreadsheet, and for the contents of those standard spreadsheets to be maintained in a database. Combined with publicly available trading and history information about the companies and shares, and an economic model, the system would enable publication in a number of different media of the investment bank's forecasts for the UK economy.

The spreadsheets were designed to have a degree of flexibility, and the calculations were saved in the database. The problem was that there was significant disagreement among the research analysts on how the system, and in particular the calculations, should work.

The challenge was that the calculations of company results appeared to be done differently by each

---

[82] Once the system has gone live, a post implementation review (PIR) is held to obtain and record lessons learned.

research analyst. Eventually the head of research appointed a committee of research analysts to finalise the calculations, and they made some headway, establishing several different types of company calculation formats, for banks, insurance and manufacturing. On the day of the presentation, the very first thing said by the head of research to his own people was - "that's not how we do it!"

Eventually the investment bank had to conclude that it did not have a standard way of calculating company results and forecasting. Fortunately the system under development was flexible enough to accommodate a late finalisation of the method.

The reality was that the investment bank did not understand this aspect of how it did its business, every analyst followed his or her own approach. The development of the system was the catalyst for building a corporate understanding of how the research department operated.

If a government department and an investment bank did not understand their business, the question is, do you?

Does your business have a business strategy? This is not a book about business strategy. I expect that you do have a business strategy, however, even if you do, the concept of strategic decay may have begun to invalidate it. Do you review it each year and renew it periodically?

Your business strategy will identify the areas where your business is to grow, and this growth will be delivered by programs and projects. Many programs and projects will involve IT systems and for this reason your business strategy is of interest to your IT supplier, or at least your IT department. It will enable prioritization of projects.

Your IT supplier, whether it is an internal or external provider, needs to be shown your business strategy in confidence, as they will no doubt provide a vital role in helping you execute the strategy. If your supplier does not know what your strategy is, it is unlikely they will be able to help make it successful.

Many years ago at the beginning of my career, a project manager expressed his exasperation with one of the line managers in our IT department. She had asked him if she should show the departmental plan to her reports and junior employees. He could not believe that she had even asked the question or thought that a plan should remain under wraps - "If no one knows what the plan is, how do we expect it to be implemented?" He would have added "Doh!" but this was before The Simpsons.

Successful prioritisation is critical to resource allocation. Prioritisation of programs and projects has to take place at an enterprise level as within each enterprise there is only one pot of resources. Resources need to be allocated, possibly over multiple financial years. A common unfortunate scenario is to divide the capital development funds to the various departments, and leave each of them with insufficient capital funds to satisfactorily progress their full program of works in the timeframe required to "catch the wave". The result may be several damp squibs.

Another common failing is to provide enough funding for one year, but not sufficient for the following years, or to demand that the program be completed by the end of the financial year, thus providing the project with a potentially impossible to meet artificial deadline.

Capital funding of programs should be undertaken at an enterprise level by ranking the programs and projects in order to ensure that there is sufficient funding for at least one priority program. The capital development budget for a corporation is determined by its capacity to borrow funds and then to use the funds to develop business ventures. The business ventures should provide a return on investment greater than a threshold that ought to be equal or higher than the corporation's historical and target return on investment. Programs which rank lower and for which funds are not available are simply not economic and, if pursued, would reduce the value and ultimate competitiveness of the entire organization. Rather than several damp squibs - the result should be at least one successful firework display.

Do you have a business plan? This plan should develop the business strategy down to an operational level describing how the business will execute on an annual basis. It describes the businesses inputs and output products, and how the resources of the enterprise are used to transform the raw material and add value to the products.

The business plan of consulting firms was once described by Sir John Harvey Jones[83] as people who borrow your watch to tell you the time. Nowadays he might have said it's about turning money into Powerpoint.

Part of the business plan at an operational level is a description of the processes that are used to turn inputs into valuable outputs.

Do you have your business processes documented? If your business processes are not written down, how do you know what you are doing? How do you know that you have an end-to-end process to deliver your product or service? How can you

---

[83] A former chairman of ICI and TV personality, and pioneer of reality TV

verify its efficiency? How can you make efficiency improvements if the process is not written down? If it's not written down, how do you know it's correct?

I was once asked to try to streamline what would nowadays be known as the process for provisioning[84] accounts on a computer system. This involved the process of applying for and being given an account to access a computer system. It involved a form. Lots of people had to look at the form and sign it. It passed through eight hands, and in some cases it was difficult to see what, if anything, was being achieved at each stage. The final stage was when Janet passed the form to Steve. I asked Steve, "Why does she give the form to you?"

"I don't know" he replied.

"What do you do with it?" I asked

"I put it in the bin."

It's amazing how many organizations have inefficient processes that defy logic. Or don't have them written down, or don't have consistency or are not understood by senior management.

---

[84] Provisioning is the process of loading the identities, roles and access rights for the users of a system. In laymans' terms it is the loading of the user names and passwords. Provisioning is a great example of misleading and obscure IT jargon.

Your business processes are the backbone of the day-to-day successful operation of your business. If documented they can be improved and made more efficient by application of processes such as business process reengineering[85], or Six Sigma[86] process improvement techniques.

Your business processes are supported by information systems. If your processes are not defined efficiently, the systems you commission may not be the most desirable or cost effective for your business. Even worse, the processes you have now may be based around your existing inefficient business systems.

If your processes are not documented, and you are dependent upon business systems, how can you change and improve your business system? Without agreed and documented processes, there is no way to validate a business systems requirements document. A business requirements document created in such an environment is largely opinion based.

---

[85] Business process reengineering (BPR) is the process of rebuilding your businesses processes from scratch to make them more efficient. BPR was devised by Michael Hammer who described it in his Harvard Business Review article – "Don't automate, obliterate".

[86] Six Sigma is a method used in business that measures the quality of a process in terms of its defects. Six sigma is a statistical measure that means only 3.4 defects per million items.

For a commercial enterprise evidence of success is often the best demonstration that you understand your business. For some government organizations, merely keeping out of the news is sufficient evidence of success.

Does your business make money? Does your business satisfy your stakeholders? Are your products sought out by your customers? How does your business compare with your competitors?

Your people are a critical indicator of how well you understand your business. Are they sought out by competitors? Do you train them regularly? Are they well paid?

If your business is one that does not have any competition, such as a monopoly service provider, perhaps a government department, then getting a realistic view on the performance of your organization can be a challenge. Organisations performing the same function can often work completely differently and a comparison of the different approaches can be valuable.

I was once in a position to compare two government departments performing the same function, one in Australia, one in the UK. The UK organisation was completely centralized and conducted transactions with citizens by post or at a post office. The

Australian organisation used a network of customer service centres in major towns. To pay for services, the most common approach adopted by citizens was to attend the service centre and pay in person. Fully 50% of all customer service transactions were simple payments that could have been done at a post office or online, or by post. Indeed many of the other transactions could have been eliminated.

At no point had any bench marking been done to determine how the organization compared with similar organisations overseas. The cost of transactions was clearly significantly higher in Australia.

Before embarking on a major new project, the best starting place is a solid understanding of the business you already have.

Do you understand what you want?

"What would you do differently next time?" asked the head of equity research to the project director responsible for the new equities research system. "I'd have one of your research analysts assigned full time on the project to ensure that we get the requirements definition correct." I remember thinking what a thoughtful answer. He continued, "only joking". It was a case of asking a stupid question to get a stupid answer, and I was not in on the joke. There was no way that a research analyst would give up his highly paid role, even for the same salary, to work as a business analyst. The only way we could get engagement with the research team was to learn to be research analysts by understanding their job, creating a process description, and then outlining the business requirements. These requirements were then validated with the research analysts by delegating sections of the document to different analysts to confirm or otherwise. It did seem to work - during a training session, after the system was complete, I heard one of the analysts point out to another a section of the system that he had helped design.

The opposite problem was encountered in a government department. The fastest way to get a promotion from the customer service centre and a pay rise was to join the business analysis team. Business analysts recruited in this way were very focused on the system and its screens and unable to abstract upwards to broader business requirements. Everything was seen in terms of the system itself, rather than the business objectives and process and legislative requirements.

Creating the business requirements for a new business system is the most critical stage in the process of creating the new system. It is very early in the software development lifecycle of the new system. Decisions made here have significant effect during the follow on stages of the project. Any error here will be amplified later in the system development. A correct set of business requirements will save time and money. An incorrect set of business requirements will waste a significant part of your budget.

Only someone who understands the business and the objectives of the business, and the business process can be expected to define the requirements for a new system.

At a client building a personalized web site, the businessperson responsible for defining the requirements had some interesting ideas. One was that the web site would display the weather in the locality where the business was based - this she saw as geographic personalization. Another large section of the requirements was devoted to automation of her own job. Every time we presented her with a draft of requirements it needed revision. Her requirements were at a very detailed screen design level. What she failed to grasp was that she needed to determine how the marketing objectives of the company were to be fulfilled in the new web site. Put bluntly, what did we need to sell to who, and how? Many months were wasted until it was realized that the wheel spinning was due to a lack of understanding of strategic objectives, and the development from these of a plan for the new web site, and a process that could be implemented in the web site to make the right offer to the right client.

The client eventually realized, with lots of prodding from the IT supplier, that what was needed was a top to bottom understanding of the requirements to bridge the gap between the strategic objectives through to the business processes and requirements. An alternative businessperson with a higher-level view of the situation was eventually substituted, and we got moving.

Choosing the correct person with the appropriate view of the business area is critical. Even more important is keeping them aligned with corporate objectives, and ensuring that they start at the top, with the objectives, and work their way down. Too many start at the bottom with a screen design. If your business analysts start with the design of the login screen, you might as well save time and money and replace them.

A chicken and egg problem is an all too common reason for starting at the bottom - after all, if we don't know what is possible, we cannot create requirements. The people writing the requirements for the first Internet banking system must have known about the Internet. There is an answer - the iterative development of requirements, from the top down.

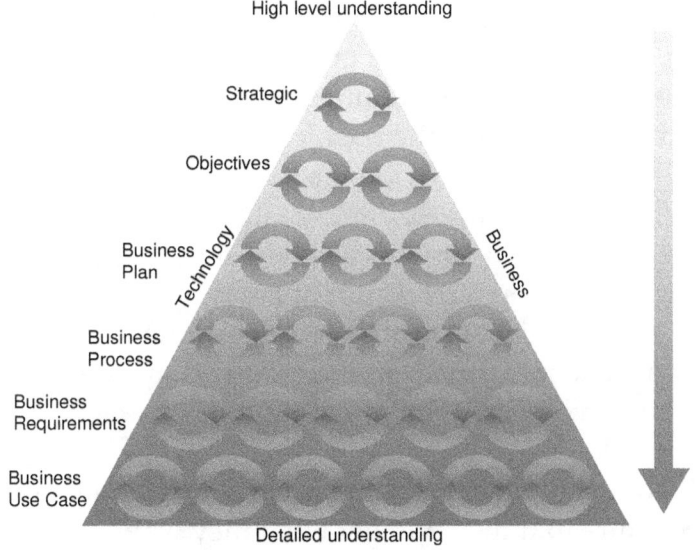

The diagram above shows how requirements can be developed top down, beginning with strategic objectives, and research about how to achieve them with available technology. As the requirements are developed and elaborated in progressively more detail, they should be reviewed with the business leadership, and IT leadership.

One way to think about the triangle is a pendulum - the pendulum swings between business and technology, cross validating one with the other as the elaboration progresses to more detail. With each swing of the pendulum, the requirements are validated by management.

Senior business leadership needs to remain in touch with the content of the requirements as they are developed. A commonly occurring scenario is that having delegated the requirements development to a junior member of the business team, the results of delegation are to provide the business leadership with more time for the immediate task of running the business. The project itself, being a longer term priority is often pushed out of the way in favour of more immediate priorities. When you next come up for air you may find that the requirements are not being developed in the direction you expected.

Keeping in touch enables your business leadership to ensure that they will get what they want.

Part of keeping in touch is about ensuring that the requirements as they are elaborated are described in a way that can be understood. Your business system requirements should be described in prose text with sentences and paragraphs, and should be readable and make sense to both the business leadership, and your IT supplier. You should avoid letting your business analysts proceed too early to technical definitions. Instead, they should produce a descriptive narrative with diagrams as necessary. Don't let them substitute bullets for sentences.

Documents should be supplemented, or be in the form of presentations that can be shared on screen, or walked through one page at a time. An increasingly popular approach is a hybrid document that uses PowerPoint to enable it to be presented, but delivers on the detail in full prose within the document itself. This hybrid document can act both as a presentation and a final document.

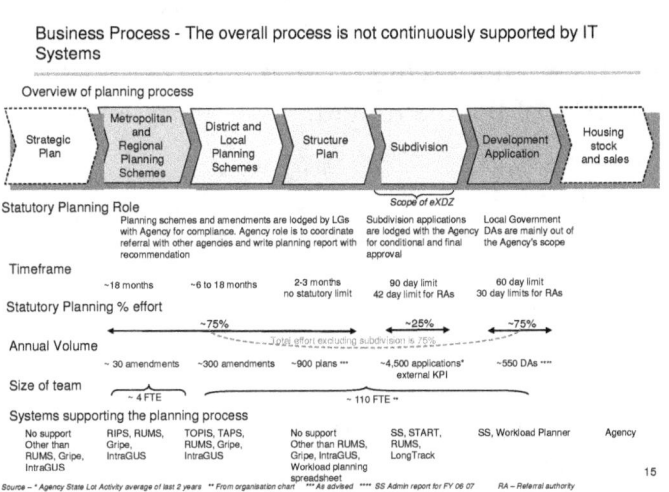

An example is shown above from one such hybrid document at the business plan stage.

If your business analysts are tempted to jump into technical detail too soon, the risk is that you will lose the ability to trace your requirements back to the process and strategy stage. A common pitfall is to commence the development of what are known as use cases[87] too early. Before this starts, you need a requirements definition that describes the system almost at the level of a film script or storyboard, so that it can be cross-referenced. More importantly it needs to be understandable by the head of the business area commissioning the system and his or her people at the coalface.

The critical take away here is that before the technical work begins your senior management must understand and accept the requirements, by reading them and having taken part in a critical presentation of the document.

---

[87] Use Cases are business requirements for a system to support a business process.

How fast and reliable does your system need to be?

You know your system needs to be fast and reliable, but just how fast does it need to be, and how should you specify this? How reliable does it need to be?

Early in my career, I was working with some researchers at an oil company. Each week they needed to send a file from the research centre to the exploration division's head office. I looked at our communications network diagram, and this showed that we did have a fixed communications link[88] with exploration division. Soon I had established a simple automated procedure for them to send the file each week. I tested it, and it was fine, but I did not test a copy of the actual file they were sending. It soon transpired that the file was huge, and the transmission time was about three days. My boss laughed at my solution when he found out, and I, too, found the outcome hilarious. It did actually satisfy the customer, but unfortunately the line was clogged up for a whole three days. From this early experience I learned the importance of performance, capacity planning and testing.

---

[88] A private permanent data link between two sites. Not often used these days.

How fast does your system need to perform? If you are planning a web based system the performance of your system directly impacts on your customers. "But performance is the IT supplier's problem!", I hear you say, "What's this got to do with us?" You are right to a degree, however, the business must specify the performance of the system in order for the IT supplier to deliver.

You need to think in terms of how fast a web page should return results to a customer. Should the page respond in 5 seconds or 10 seconds? Is that duration an average or a maximum? A reasonable way to specify response times is statistically based with 98% of response times, two standard deviations from the mean, being within the target for web page response time. You need to think also in terms of a given maximum number of customers at any one time.

The faster the required performance, the higher the cost of the business system as the more hardware[89] and bandwidth[90] will be needed to support it. How reliable and available should your system be? Again, this is not a problem solely for your IT

---

[89] The actual computers.

[90] The capacity of a data channel in terms of bits per second, or more likely mega bits per second.

supplier. A common business response is to demand that a system be available 24 hours a day, seven days a week. This comes at a significantly steeper price than a system available 9am to 5pm Monday to Friday.

Planned availability is one thing, but you should also consider unplanned outages. Imagine for a moment that a physical disaster destroys your machine room[91], leaving everything else intact. How long would it take to restore your business system to operation? For some companies the answer would be to get the back up tapes[92] and system architecture documents, order new hardware, install the software and recommission the systems as they were before the disaster. This might take months. At the other end of the spectrum, banks are required to provide return to operation within a few seconds by switching to backup disaster recovery systems[93]. This clearly is a significant expense. Your role as a businessperson is to determine how quickly your business system needs to return to operation, and how much you want to spend. Your

---

[91] The room where you keep your servers.

[92] Data security for some systems is provided by backing up the data periodically to tape or other media, and storing it off site in a secure location. Nowadays storage is often backed up continuously to a remote site.

[93] Disaster recovery (DR) systems are systems that are on standby to takeover if the primary operational system becomes unavailable.

IT supplier is responsible for costing and delivering the disaster recovery solution.

Be aware of performance and reliability, it directly affects customers perception of your company, and it costs money.

Why does your business need this system?

"Why on earth have you spent $5 million building this?" asked the oil company CEO, to the consternation of the oil company software developer. He was demonstrating an expert system he had built using Prolog[94] to classify conodonts. Conodonts are obscure microscopic fossil teeth that are used in the oil industry as markers for particular stratigraphic layers. They also indicated the degree to which the rocks had been cooked. More cooking meant more oil, and more oil means more money and so conodont identification was a valuable skill. Geologists did not even know what the animal they came from looked like, but nevertheless had built up a massive store of information. The researcher explained, "By putting this knowledge into a rules engine that could identify the conodonts, well, it would be useful." Unfortunately the CEO was having none of it. "But conodont experts only cost me about $100k a year, and we only employ two or three. Plus it will probably need a conodont expert to operate it. I could save more money by sacking you." The researcher kept his job, and it probably did not help that the CEO had once been rejected for a job at the research centre. But it did highlight the

---

[94] A computer programming language for expert systems.

need for business cases for expensive software developments.

Your situation is different, you know why you need your system. You have a business case that demonstrates why. But where does your business case fit into your company's overall plan to maintain and grow its market share? Efficient businesses seek to grow by capturing greater market share, or by developing the market by introducing new products, or by entering new markets. To do this a business needs to compare the value of the new business opportunity with its existing business, and other possible business opportunities. Other factors need to be taken into account, such as the forecast growth of the current or new market, the skills available to the company, the fit between the existing business and the new business. Frequently business cases will be about advancing an existing business.

It does sometimes happen that a business steps into a completely new area. Jaguar Cars started out manufacturing motorcycle side-cars[95] in 1922, and progressively worked its way through producing improved body panels for existing cars, to buying car chassis and building the body, to commissioning and then building its own chassis and body, and

---

[95] See the cartoon film Wallace & Gromit to get a better appreciation of side-cars.

finally designing and building its own cars. Each stage would have required a business case that justified the move into a more profitable area.

Nokia[96] likewise began as a paper mill in 1902, growing as an industrial conglomerate in such areas as power generation, cable manufacturing, electronics and finally, mobile phones. In the 1990s it eventually sold all the businesses not connected with mobile communications. Each step change required a business case. Most companies, yours included, do not make such large changes, but the principle is the same, there must be an economic case for the new investment.

Of course, your reasons for your new system may not be to enter a new market - there may be regulatory reasons for the business case, or it may be a mandatory activity of a government department. Nevertheless, the same financial pressures apply. In the case of regulatory requirements, the business case benefits might be the costs saved by not having to paying fines for non-compliance. In the case of a government spending department the overall business case might be more complex than a financial analysis as it will involve political factors in the supply of services to citizens in exchange for their vote.

---

[96] As of 2014 Nokia is probably wishing it had stayed in the paper mill business.

Nevertheless, it will involve supplying the service at the lowest acceptable cost.

Your business case will include a financial analysis that shows the benefits and costs over a five-year period. Taken together, a typical business project will show an overall cash flow that typically will show some early costs to establish the new platform, followed by a benefits stream that pays for the costs of the new platform and delivers additional value, or profits to the business.

A simplified example is shown below

Net Present Value for a project						
	Year 1	Year 2	Year 3	Year 4	Year 5	Total
Costs	$1,000,000	$10,000	$10,000	$10,000	$10,000	$1,040,000
Benefits	$0	$500,000	$500,000	$500,000	$500,000	$2,000,000
Cashflow	-$1,000,000	$490,000	$490,000	$490,000	$490,000	$960,000
Cumulative cashflow	-$1,000,000	-$510,000	-$20,000	$470,000	$960,000	
Net Present Value	$269,602					

The first stage in deciding if your project has legs, is to answer two questions:

How quickly do I get a return on investment, or in other words, when is the break-even point? Does it have a positive *net present value*?

The break-even point represents the point in the cash flow where the business has got its money back. Ideally this should be within two or three years. In the example above the break even point appears to be very early in the fourth year.

The net present value, or NPV, of an investment tells you what the investment would be worth if you had all the future payments available now. This is not the same as adding them up. If you had $100 now, if would be worth $118 in one year's time if the interest rate were 18%. Another way to look at this, is that $118 in one year's time is worth $100 in the present. It's worth less. The net present value of $118 one year in the future is just $100. If you had $100 one year from now, it would be worth $84.74 in the present time. This is its net present value (NPV).

A stream of future values can each have a value in the present determined, and the sum of these is the NPV for the future cash flow.

Why is the interest rate, or internal rate of return set at 18%? You may think 18% rather high. This is a standard set by accounting bodies, and is based upon the highest value in the recent history of interest rates.

How can we use the NPV value? Well, first of all it should be positive, and in addition should be at least 40% higher than the total expenditure - this is your business margin, after all, you don't work just to get your money back.

Your business case must compete with other

business cases in the same organisation for a limited supply of capital. In a typical organisation business cases would be ranked according to economic benefit, using such measures as net present value, and payback period. Then a second stage of selection would take place, to select projects according to capital available. Of course a project business case with a very high net present value might require more capital than the corporation can obtain, and so would not be feasible. Those projects that are feasible are the highest ranked projects by NPV whose capital requirements are within the available capital budget.

Consider the following projects that are being considered by a corporation that is able to borrow $15 million. It cannot afford project 7 even thought it has the highest net present value, as it would have to borrow above its limit. However projects 3, 4, 5 and 6 together will cost a total of $15 million, and have a net present value of about $4.5 million. Projects 1 and 2 miss out as they offer a lower net present value, and for the purpose of this exercise are therefore lower priority and they would take the capital requirements over the $15 million limit.

	Project 1	Project 2	Project 3	Project 4	Project 5	Project 6	Project 7
NPV	$75,000	$130,000	$269,601	$600,000	$1,200,000	$2,400,000	$4,800,000
Costs	$250,000	$500,000	$1,000,000	$2,000,000	$4,000,000	$8,000,000	$16,000,000

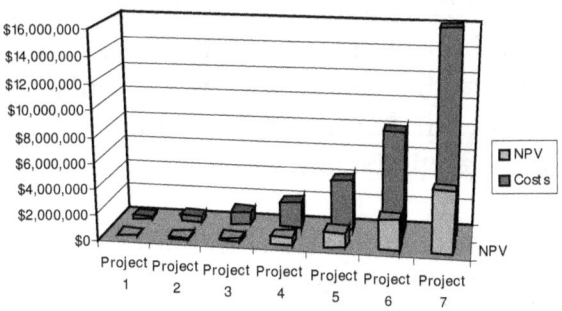

A common objection by the project sponsor of a project such as project 2, is that project 2 is an essential pre-requisite for project 4, and as a result project 2 should also go ahead. If project 4 depends upon project 2, then they should either be merged into one project, or there should be a program business case that justifies both projects. As you can see, if this is the case, then project 3 will have to be cancelled to pay for project 2. Of course project 6 may be dependent on project 3, and so you can see why budgeting is so complex.

If project 5 suffers an overrun of costs, then projects lower down the pecking order may have to be cancelled or delayed.

A question often arises as to how the capital development budget is set in corporations. The capital available comprises retained profits after distribution and taxation, and borrowings. In most corporations, borrowing is used to fund expansion and the amount that can be borrowed is subject to limits similar to those that anyone applying for a home mortgage will be familiar with.

Leveraging corporate equity with borrowing is subject to limits that are typically set by a combination of share market appetite for the degree of leverage, and the market for bonds. Currently many corporations have a leverage ratio between 0.5 and 1. In other words, they are typically borrowing up to an equivalent of the capital available, instead of issuing new shares to obtain the capital. But the details of this are beyond the scope of this work.

Clearly project business cases in corporations need to be subject to the utmost competitive scrutiny, as the company itself is in open market competition. If a survival of the fittest approach is not applied to project business cases, then the entire company itself may no longer be able to keep pace with the competition. Your future business is based on past and present business cases, they are not just there to justify spending on IT systems.

Mistakes in business cases are not uncommon. Take an example at a very large bank, where one businessperson had an extraordinarily good business case. The NPV was enormous. The proposed business was the online sales of unit trusts through an online banking system. The benefits were large, and the costs were being elaborated ready for submission to the bank's business case team. The IT supplier's project manager was amending the cost estimates when he glanced at the benefits side of the business case spreadsheet. Something was not quite right. The business had included the revenue as the benefit, whereas the benefit should only have been the fee on the revenue - approximately 2%. At this point the NPV began to look very ordinary.

At another firm a key part of the benefit for a business case was a reduction in costs for distributing news by using an electronic newsletter. The company had been planning to start a conventional newsletter, and the savings in printing and postage costs were enormous. These savings represented about 80% of the benefits. Unfortunately as these costs were not yet incurred, the only benefits that should really have been attributed to the project were the benefits from the proposed electronic newsletter. As a result, a project went ahead that should have been stopped. The same organisation found that the benefits that would become available as a result of a new system could not be used to justify the new system as the benefits had been earmarked to pay for the increase in staffing in the marketing department. As a result, they ended up inadvertently double counting benefits.

Which brings us to benefits management. It is not uncommon to find that benefits in business cases are never realised, or that the same benefit gets re-used in many different business cases. For instance, in one organization it was found that if every saving in staffing costs was realized, the organization would have to shed more people than it employed.

Benefits management means that business cases need to be managed and reviewed as a group to ensure that they are consistent as a group, After all, as a group, they may well represent the future success of the entire organization. In addition, benefits management should take place over the lifetime of the benefits, to ensure that they are realized. In particular, if costs savings are anticipated as part of a business case, it is appropriate that budgets are seen to be reduced in line with the business cases.

When developing a business case, identifying the benefits is often the most challenging part. Often pressure on the cost side to improve a marginal business case could be equally applied to the benefits side of the equation. Business cases often include both tangible and intangible benefits, and one area for attention is turning the intangibles into tangible benefits. Intangible benefits are best considered poorly understood tangible benefits and can often be developed into tangible financial benefits.

An example of the financial components of a business case is shown below

Example business case financial plan						
	Total	Year 1	Year 2	Year 3	Year 4	Year 5
Benefits	**$1,945,907**					
Staff savings	$836,725		$200,000	$206,000	$212,180	$218,545
Increased margin	$900,000		$100,000	$200,000	$300,000	$300,000
Reduced costs	$209,181		$50,000	$51,500	$53,045	$54,636
Costs	**-$1,224,005**					
Hardware costs	-$100,000	-$100,000				
Project hardware costs	-$20,000	-$20,000				
Software licensing	-$53,091	-$10,000	-$10,300	-$10,609	-$10,927	-$11,255
Project software costs	-$20,000	-$20,000				
Project resources	-$500,000	-$500,000				
Operational costs	-$530,914	-$100,000	-$103,000	-$106,090	-$109,273	-$112,551
Cash flow		-$750,000	$236,700	$340,801	$445,025	$449,376
Cumulative Cash flow		-$750,000	-$513,300	-$172,499	$272,526	$721,902
CPI		3%	3%	3%	3%	3%
NPV	**$167,788**					
Internal Rate of Return	18%					

There are two key components to this, the benefits and the costs. Getting a comprehensive list of each is a critical stage in the business case. As a businessperson you will be aware that benefits tend to be overstated, and costs underestimated. Producing a comprehensive list, and considering all the costs and benefits over five years will enable the likelihood of this common error scenario to be reduced.

The benefits list should comprise all possible

savings as a result of the new platform, including staff cost savings, reduced cost of operations, and additional margin (not revenue) as a result of the new platform. These should of course be described in the business case narrative. Typically you, as the business, will be supplying the list of benefits. The most common cause of overstating benefits is in the area of increased margin, as the increase in revenue, or sales, is much more challenging to predict than the savings.

The costs of the new platform comprise the costs of development and ongoing technical operation, plus the business costs of launch and the ongoing business costs of operation. Your IT supplier should provide the technical costs. Your IT supplier should work closely with your IT operations department to ensure that all ongoing costs are included, and you should verify the costs yourself.

A comprehensive workshop needs to be undertaken to review both the costs and benefits with all parties who contributed components. The principle that your IT supplier has been here many times before should apply and they may be able to contribute questions about the benefits.

Your business case will proceed through a series of development stages, or iterations. Each time the information in it, particularly the costs, will become more accurate. Although the steps may have different names in the various methodologies, in outline the steps are as follows.

The initiative stage is where the business has identified a new business opportunity or cost saving measure. In order to determine whether to proceed, an estimate of the costs is required. This cost estimate is obtained from your IT supplier, and is known as either a "ball park" estimate or a "rough order of magnitude" estimate. The ballpark estimate is based upon the supplier's previous experience of similar systems. You may want to get several different ballpark estimates from different sources. Estimates of costs at this stage are unlikely to be more accurate than plus 100% and minus 50%. Your benefits estimates are likely to have similar levels of inaccuracy. The purpose of the ballpark estimate is to decide if it is worth proceeding to the concept stage. Because the cost of the initiative stage is very low, it is usually undertaken as an expense of day-to-day business operations.

If the initiative is worth pursuing, then it passes to the concept stage. In the concept stage a high level outline of the requirements and a possible solution option are created. In this way your IT supplier is able to provide costs based upon an indication of the requirements and possible solution. Often the approach used for estimating is identical to that used for the next stage, the only difference being the level of detail in the requirements. Your business case should be refined and reviewed at this stage to verify that it is still worth proceeding. Be aware that a decision not to proceed should be a realistic option.

The blue print stage estimate is a high level estimate, much more accurate then previous estimates, as it is based upon detailed requirements and an architectural design based upon a chosen solution option. A revision to costs will be made at this stage. Again, the business should be ready to review these changes. The business should maintain an open mind about the continued viability of the project, especially if costs have increased significantly.

If the build of your solution is proceeding through a number of stages or iterations, then your supplier may be able to use a bottom up estimating technique. They will be able to use the actual costs from the previous stage or iteration of the project, and use these to estimate accurately each individual component. This is known as bottom up estimating, and is typically the most accurate. It is worth adjusting the business case again, if these estimates become available.

At each of these stages the business should reconsider the business case and be prepared to accept the costs presented and to take appropriate action depending upon the change to net present value and pay back period. The business understanding of the benefits may also change over time, and with each stage of the project, the business case should be revised and reviewed by the board.

Refining and pricing the solution

Once you have gathered your business requirements, your next stage is to refine the requirements and to create solution options. Business requirements typically need refining in order to optimise the cost of the solution against the benefits of the solution. A common scenario is to find that the most expensive components of the solution do not deliver the most benefit. By refining the solution we are able to ensure that the solution is cost effective. Think of it as applying the 80/20[97] rule. If we can get 80% of the benefits for 20% of the cost, we can make a good business case better, or make a bad business case possible.

Your business requirements are just that, they are not the design, just a starting point for the solution. At one client site a business analyst who had defined the requirements was surprised by what we were going to do next - to refine the requirements by turning them into a catalogue or shopping list, with priorities and complexity estimates against each item. This enables the business to work with its IT supplier to determine which requirements

---

[97] The Pareto principle states that typically we get 80% of the effect from 20% of the causes. Pareto in 1906 noted that he got 80% of his peas from 20% of the peapods in his garden.

become part of the solution. This was a novel point to the business analyst, who thought that all the requirements would become part of the system. Not necessarily so, as sometimes requirements are dropped after their individual cost benefit is identified.

The process is to take a catalogue of the requirements and to prioritise them according to "essential", "high", "medium", "low" and "nice to have". The choice of five different categories allows the possibility of a nice normal bell curve to be the outcome. The next stage is for the application architect of your IT supplier to estimate the relative complexity of the requirements.

You should get a result that looks like this, only written in English:

ID	Requirement title	Requirement definition	Business Priority	Complexity
1	Requirement 1	Lorem ipsum dolor sit amet, consectetur adipisicing elit,	1 Essential	2 Medium
2	Requirement 2	sed do eiusmod tempor incididunt ut labore et dolore magna aliqua	4 Low	1 High
3	Requirement 3	Ut enim ad minim veniam, quis nostrud exercitation ullamco laboris nisi ut aliquip ex ea commodo consequat.	3 Mediium	3 Low
4	Requirement 4	Duis aute irure dolor in reprehenderit in voluptate velit	3 Mediium	2 Medium
5	Requirement 5	esse cillum dolore eu fugiat nulla pariatur.	5 Nice to have	1 High

ID	Requirement title	Requirement definition	Business Priority	Complexity
6	Requirement 6	Excepteur sint occaecat cupidatat non proident	2 High	2 Medium
7	Requirement 7	sunt in culpa qui officia deserunt mollit anim id est laborum	5 Nice to have	3 Low
etc ...		...	...	...

Only in a realistic situation, you should have far more requirements in your list.

By sorting the requirements by complexity and business priority, it is possible to get a list like the following:

ID	Requirement title	Requirement definition	Business Priority	Complexity
2	Requirement 2	sed do eiusmod tempor incididunt ut labore et dolore magna aliqua	4 Low	1 High
5	Requirement 5	esse cillum dolore eu fugiat nulla pariatur.	5 Nice to have	1 High
1	Requirement 1	Lorem ipsum dolor sit amet, consectetur adipisicing elit,	1 Essential	2 Medium
6	Requirement 6	Excepteur sint occaecat cupidatat non proident	2 High	2 Medium
4	Requirement 4	Duis aute irure dolor in reprehenderit in voluptate velit	3 Mediium	2 Medium
3	Requirement 3	Ut enim ad minim veniam, quis nostrud exercitation ullamco laboris nisi ut aliquip ex ea commodo consequat.	3 Mediium	3 Low
7	Requirement 7	sunt in culpa qui officia deserunt mollit anim id est laborum	5 Nice to have	3 Low

ID	Requirement title	Requirement definition	Business Priority	Complexity
etc ...	...		...	...

This shows at the top that one of the high complexity and therefore potentially expensive requirements is only a nice to have. So if you want to save money, you can get rid of it now. An alternative approach is to create phases or releases or iterations and you can put the lower priority, higher complexity requirements into a later release.

Of course you can repeat this shopping list exercise at a later stage when you have developed your requirements into use cases and you can estimate the actual cost of each use case. This will provide a better insight into relative cost benefits.

Obviously this approach has its drawbacks, as sometimes something that the business sees as low priority is in fact essential to the operation of the business system even though it is rather boring.

So now you have your prioritised list of refined requirements, what comes next?

Now is the time for your IT supplier's application architects to become involved with both the requirements and the enterprise architecture. This is the critical part of the blueprint stage. The application architects need to take the requirements and devise a series of solution options based on the enterprise architecture. The options represent different ways of implementing the solution. Each solution will have good points and bad points, and the outcome of their work should be a short presentation that shows the good points and bad points of each. These points should be in the nature of requirements coverage, alignment with your existing systems and enterprise architecture, future proofing and cost.

One key aspect of their solution options should be "buy versus build". If your requirements represent a common area of business, or if you have a lot of similar competitors, there is a likelihood that a software package exists that can support many of your requirements. If this is so, then economics dictates that the software package will be less expensive, so long as you do not attempt to over customise the package. The package will inevitably be less expensive for two reasons. Firstly, for a software package to be competitive with homegrown solutions the package must cost less. Secondly, by buying a package you are effectively sharing the cost of building a solution with the supplier's other customers, plus the cost of their profit margin. Buy before build is industry recommended practice.

One client was a company that sold package holidays. They had a software development project delivering a solution intended to replace its existing systems that had been ongoing for around three years. The client was being held hostage by the developers who did not want the project to end. While exploring solutions to their 95% completion problem, one aspect that was obvious about the business was that the package holiday business was a common one. While I knew nothing about how the business worked I was sure that there had to be suitable software packages out there. It turned out that the client had looked at packages but had found them too expensive. However, they did not have a record of the costs to date of the existing development. Probably the cost to date exceeded the cost of a package, but there was no way for them to find out.

The solution options presentation should describe each option and its merits and provide a recommendation that can later be costed in more detail. This presentation should be made to the key business owners, and senior representatives of the business's IT function and IT supplier. It's an opportunity to ask questions and clarify the direction.

You should be enquiring about the extent to which the solution options are based on conservative technology or are they "bleeding edge[98]"? Are they

---

[98] A pun on leading edge. Being on the bleeding edge is the result of using something too new and untested.

high risk? If so, why? Are special skills needed to build them, and are those skills available? How are the options aligned with existing technology used within the organisation? How do the options interface with existing systems, and finally what are the relative costs and timeframes? Your IT supplier should be ready and able to answer these questions.

You also need to consider the impact that losing your new system would have on your business. What would be the cost to your business of each hour and day of lost operation? If the cost is significant, your solution needs to consider disaster recovery, and the business continuity plan to keep your business going until the system is restored. The cost of these may be significant.

The next two items that are needed in the costing journey are the business requirements use cases and the detailed architecture.

Business requirements use cases describe the external functions of the system from the outside of the system. The use cases describe the content of the screens, the data and how people use the screens. Although written in a standard form they should be understandable to the business.

The detailed architecture document defines the solution and includes the definition of the environments needed comprising hardware, licensed software, and a high-level component diagram of the system that will be built.

Once these two key documents are in place, most IT suppliers will be able to determine estimated costs to within about 30% to 50%. To do this, the use cases are assessed as described earlier and the number of use cases at each level of complexity is used to determine the man-days required to build the system. From here it is possible to determine the people needed, the timeframe and hence the costs and delivery date. The process is shown below:

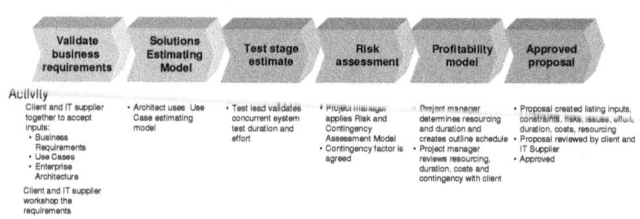

Typical software development estimating process

From a business perspective there are two ways to approach cost, time and materials or fixed price.

In the familiar time and materials approach, the

supplier provides full details on how it will deliver the solution, and bills for the work on a monthly basis. Of course, the problem here is that if the IT supplier has made any errors of judgement, the additional costs lie with you, the client.

Fixed price is just that - the IT supplier provides a fixed price for the work, which is fine in theory, but there is an up front additional cost, and a potential sting in the tail. In order to offer a fixed price, your IT supplier will introduce a risk contingency factor into the pricing that will drive up the price by a percentage depending on the risk that the IT supplier foresees. In effect you as the business are paying an insurance premium. Fixed price costs more. In addition, suppliers may use an additional protection measure - they may include assumptions about their understanding of the risk they are taking on. If these assumptions are broken, then the expectation is more money will be requested from the client.

Fixed price is useful when you are commissioning a high-risk software development, but is not useful for many areas of straight consulting, such as business requirements or testing.

In summary, to get the most cost effective solution, you need to work flexibly with your IT supplier to identify the optimum set of your requirements, and the best technology platform on which to build. You also need to select with care the most suitable form of contract.

Proof of concept, prototypes, pilots and iterations

The business system you are about to build is a relatively high-risk exercise, particularly if you follow the conventional path of defining the requirements, designing the solution and then building and testing it. While this approach does work and is still used, it does have the deficiency that the delivery of the product takes place at the end of the project, and the risks are still present until this final delivery.

Increasingly the practice is to try to reduce the risk early, by delivering some part of the solution early. There are two main types of risk that can be reduced, one risk is technical - will the selected software enable us to deliver the system? The other is business - do we have a clear understanding of what we want?

There are numerous early delivery approaches that are available to reduce risk.

A "proof of concept" is often used where there is uncertainty around an aspect of the technology. A good example was at a bank where the credit card system was being outsourced. As a consequence payment messages, which previously entered the bank's security perimeter[99], would now have to also exit the bank's network perimeter security service and cross the supplier's security perimeter. As performance of credit card transactions was a paramount requirement, and indeed subject to independent standards, it had to be proved that the additional security, in the form of an extra firewall[100], would not slow the messages down. The technique used was to develop a system that simulated sending and receiving the card messages at the bank's maximum Christmas Eve load, to ensure that performance was not impacted. Before the project was really even past the concept stage, this risk was removed from the register with the successful conclusion of the proof of concept. In fact, another four proof of concept exercises were undertaken to reduce risk in other components of the solution. These proof of concept exercises are expensive, but by undertaking them early any cost impacts can be identified early and used in the decision making process.

Clients often ask, "Will you reuse the proof of

---

[99] A set of highly secure firewalls that surround a bank's computer systems. The security perimeter protects the bank's computers against unauthorised access.

[100] A firewall is a specialised computer that examines computer communications to ensure that only permitted types and sources of data communications can pass through.

concept in the production system?" - the answer is always no - it will not have been built to production standards, just sufficient to test the problem area. The proof of concept code may well be used by the developer as a starting point for the production code, so it will not be entirely discarded.

A "prototype" takes place earlier in the lifecycle, and is typically a non-functional demonstration of the key screens in the business system. This enables the business owners and possibly eventually the business users of the system to see what the system will look like and to provide comments on how it can be improved. Often a lot of important feedback can be gathered about the system before any real development work is done. Prototypes can be paper based - that is a set of wire frame screens can be quickly drawn and printed out, or shown on a projector in order to get feedback during workshops about the design. This enables requirements to be ironed out before a lot of money has been expended on the system. Prototypes can be very low cost and provide very high value, yet unfortunately they can often be seen as time wasting.

A variation on the prototype is the usability study, where key screens are created on paper, sometimes by a design firm, and variations tested with potential customers to get their feedback. Surprising and valuable results can be obtained this way.

A "pilot scheme" is a release of an early version of the system to a small group of hopefully friendly business customers to get early feedback. In the web portal business it has become known as a soft launch - the system is there and in use but it has not been widely announced or launched. This enables the business to use the early feedback to enhance the eventual product launch.

A "thin slice" is another way of testing your concept. In this approach a functioning slice of the production system is built from screens through application services and database. This can be used to demonstrate the look and feel of a key aspect of the system, reduce technical risk, and even improve the estimation of the rest of the system.

"Iterative development" sometimes known as agile development is an increasingly used approach that delivers some early results, and provides an opportunity for the business to provide early commentary on early releases of the system, in order to include refinements and improvements to the requirements. The approach is to deliver the system in a series of short fixed period releases sometimes called "sprints". The requirements, design and software are incrementally delivered and tested. Feedback from the business is used to improve the next iteration. The first iterations will be released to test, but later iterations will be business releases, with each successive release adding more functions. This approach was used to deliver the teller system at a major bank in 11 iterations of about three months each.

Iterative development is a mainstream approach, and requires significant maturity on the part of the business and IT supplier, and also has a significant management overhead. However, it has proven its worth by reducing the risk of development and providing an early view of the business solution.

All of these approaches can potentially reduce the risk on your project, by early examination and mitigation of the risk. Together with your IT supplier you should consider these options.

Monitoring your project

Many business people who commission a project
find themselves receiving bad news, but even
worse, is the way it is sometimes delivered, as a
complete surprise. The key to avoiding surprises is
a mixture of risk management, issue management,
tracking and control, and periodic reporting.

Risk management is key to understanding the many
ways that things can go wrong on your project.
Significant effort needs to be put into risk
management, to articulate the ways things can go
off the rails, how likely this is, and what's to be done
if it happens. Early in the project, the IT supplier's
project manager needs to meet with the business
people commissioning the system and discuss the
risks that are being run. As discussed earlier in the
chapter, "The nature of the problem", building a
business system is very different to the business you
normally undertake in your office. Therefore you
need to be aware of the risks that you are running,
and this may even assist you, if you do the risk
review early enough, to decide if fixed price is the
right choice for your system. Each risk needs to be
understood and accepted by the business. It's you
that is running the risk not your IT supplier, a point
that is often overlooked by business executives. The
point of having the risks recorded is that the IT
supplier can come to you when the risk eventuates

and say, "Look, that problem we told you about, well it transpired, and may we have more time and money?" Ideally your risk log should include not only a qualitative measure of risks, but also a quantitative measure showing the cost to the project if each risk eventuates, and the probability. The overall probability adjusted cost of risk on the project can be easily established, and this dollar amount should be your contingency for risk. The size of the contingency budget is often a surprise to the business. The impact of the overall size of the budget across a corporation's entire program of work is significant.

You also need a contingency budget for change[101], and this should be separate to the risk contingency budget. None of these contingencies should be used without the approval of the business.

Issues, or problems as they arise, need to be documented and tracked to ensure visibility to the business commissioning the system, and to monitor how they are managed.

The project's schedule needs to be tracked, showing how the project is completing each product, and the forecast completion date, and overall estimated cost to complete.

---

[101] A budget that the customer should set aside to pay for any changes that the customer wishes to make to the requirements.

Your project manager should report periodically, and how often this is done depends upon a number of factors, including the length of the project and the news cycle. The news cycle in most organisations is monthly, this being the financial reporting cycle. As a consequence the project reporting cycle should be some whole multiple or whole fraction of one month. Typically one month is too long a reporting period. On the other hand one week is to short. A fortnight is closer to the ideal, however, this is not a regular fraction of a month. My suggestion for your consideration is that the typical reporting period is twice a month.

What should a report consist of? Many organisations these days have standard reporting templates but my suggestion to you is this - let your project manager agree a format with you, and expect the format to change during the life of the project. The basic information you need is, what progress have we made creating products? How does this compare with costs and time schedule? What issues are we dealing with? How has the risk profile changed? What have we spent to date? What is the current forecast completion date and cost?

After the project

After the solution has been delivered and the new business system is in operation, there is one final step, and that is to conduct a post implementation review. A post implementation review gathers the good and bad points of the projects and creates a list of lessons learned and recommended actions for future projects. This is corporate learning, without it there is a strong possibility of your business repeating the same mistakes over and over again.

The post implementation review should be facilitated and written by people not involved in the project. The reason is that various participants on the project will almost certainly have conflicting views as to what was good and bad, and it's important to have all the views represented. Do not attempt to form a consensus about lessons learned where it is clear that agreement cannot be reached.

The lessons learned and recommended actions should be maintained in an enterprise register, so that the information can be communicated to those responsible for managing projects. A business that can learn lessons is a business that is more likely to grow.

Epilogue

This modest distillation of some experience dealing with information systems projects is in many ways what just about anyone would tell you on the subject, if they had time, and part of the reason I have written this down is that so often when a situation arises on a project, the project manager is in the thick of it, and his advice is often overlooked in favour of someone whose main credibility is that they are not involved. After all, the person reporting an issue is often seen as the cause of it, and for some, the solution is to shoot the messenger. By writing down some of the classical problems and some possible solutions, my hope is that the poor messenger is removed from the immediate fray, and can point to previously written down suggestions for solutions.

Hopefully this advice will enable you to get your new business system in less time for less money.

The end